WONDERS OF THE WORLD

MADAGASCAR

Martin J. Gutnik
& Natalie Browne-Gutnik

Technical Consultant

Roderic B. Mast
Vice President, Conservation International

Primary Photographer
Walt Anderson

RAINTREE
STECK-VAUGHN
P U B L I S H E R S
The Steck-Vaughn Company

Austin, Texas

A production of B&B Publishing, Inc.

Editor – Jean B. Black
Photo Editor – Margie Benson
Computer Specialist – Katy O'Shea
Interior Design – Scott Davis

Raintree Steck-Vaughn Publishing Staff

Project Editor – Helene Resky
Project Manager – Joyce Spicer

LIBRARY OF CONGRESS CATALOGING-IN-PUBLICATION DATA

Gutnik, Martin J.
    Madagascar / Martin J. Gutnik, Natalie Browne-Gutnik
       p. cm. — (Wonders of the world)
    Includes bibliographical references (p.) and index.
    ISBN 0-8114-6372-9
    1. Natural history — Madagascar — Juvenile literature. 2. Madagascar —
Juvenile literature. 3. Nature conservation — Madagascar — Juvenile literature.
[1. Natural history — Madagascar. 2. Madagascar.] I. Browne-Gutnik, Natalie.
II. Title. III. Series.
QH195.M2G88 1995
508.691 — dc20

94-41785
CIP
AC

Cover photo	Title page photo	Table of Contents page photo
Rice paddies in November	**Traveler's palm tree on a riverbank**	**A lemur in the Berenty Reserve**

PHOTO SOURCES

Cover Photo: © David Austen/Tony Stone Worldwide

© Walt Anderson: 1, 5, 7 top, 8, 9, 10 both, 13 right, 15, 17, 18 bottom, 19 both, 20 bottom, 23 both, 25 both, 26 top, 27, 29 left, 30, 32 both, 33 all, 34, 35 both, 36, 37 both, 38, 39 both, 41 left, 42, 45 right, 46 top, 47, 50 both, 51 both, 52 both, 54, 56 both, 57, 58 top, 59, 60
Conservation International: 4
Conservation International/©Haroldo Castro: 3, 9 inset, 16, 41 bottom
Conservation International/©Patrick Daniels: 58 right

Conservation International/©Roderic B. Mast: 7 right
Conservation International/©Russ Mittermeier: 29 bottom, 40, 46 bottom, 53 left, 55
David Haring/Duke University Primate Center: 45 bottom
© Frans Lanting/Minden Pictures: 12
© 1992 Eugene G. Schulz: 6, 13 top, 14 both, 18 top, 20 left, 22, 24, 26 left, 28, 31, 43, 44 both, 48, 49, 53 top

Printed and bound in the United States of America.
1 2 3 4 5 6 7 8 9 VH 99 98 97 96 95 94

Table of Contents

The baobab tree is an easily recogniz-able symbol of Madagascar. This tree may have a trunk up to 30 feet (9 m) in diameter.

One of a Kind

Madagascar is like no other place on Earth. On this strange piece of land, 75 percent of the plant and animal life is unique to the island. Why are living things so different there? Why did evolution follow such a different course from the rest of the world?

Madagascar, the fourth-largest island in the world, covers 226,658 square miles (587,041 sq km). It lies in the Indian Ocean southeast of Africa. Even the way it was formed, its geologic history, makes Madagascar different. Many of Earth's islands are the result of volcanic eruptions and coral reefs. Madagascar, however, was once part of a continental landmass—hence its base of granite and gneiss rock.

In the early 1900s, German meteorologist A.L. Wegener proposed a new theory called "continental drift." The Earth's continents were once a single landmass. He called this landmass Pangaea, after the Greek word meaning "Earth goddess." According to Wegener, about 180 million years ago, this vast piece of land broke into two pieces—Laurasia to the north and Gondwanaland to the south. The giant continent of Gondwanaland was probably made up of what is now South America, Antarctica, Africa, India, and Australia. He called the large body of water that separated the two lands the Sea of Tethys.

During that same period, geologists have found evidence of massive geologic activity that caused major changes on Earth. Violent earthquakes moved the ground. Volcanoes spewed hot lava and created new land forms. The resulting changes led to an amazing alteration of life on Earth.

Ocean surf breaks on Precambrian rocks at Roclandes, St. Luce, Madagascar. These rocks were formed billions of years ago during the Precambrian era, the earliest period of Earth's history.

Approximately 180 million years ago, during the Jurassic period of the Cretaceous era, the climate on Earth was cold. Reptiles reigned during this period. Many land dinosaurs were giants. Triceratops had a huge horn; *tyrannosaurus* had a huge head; and *stegosaurus* had a double row of upright bony plates along its back. *Brontosaurus* was a vegetarian. *Iguanodon* was a large two-footed lizard. Flying reptiles known as pterodactyls were the ancestors of modern birds. The sea provided a habitat for mosasaurs, ichthyosaurs, and plesiosaurs. None of these species exist today—they are all extinct.

Some ancient species we might recognize today include crocodiles and turtles, gigantic lizards, and snakes large enough to swallow a small elephant. Some small, primitive mammals developed. Their current descendants are known as marsupials. Birds appeared during the late Jurassic period. The archaeopteryx bridged the gap between reptiles and birds.

Gondwanaland eventually broke into pieces due to many strong earthquakes. The movement of the Earth's crust along its mantle continued, causing landmasses to drift farther apart. Most of the newly formed continents drifted no more than 1 inch (2.5 cm) a year, except India, which may have drifted 2 inches (5 cm) yearly. Even now, the Earth's landmasses drift at a slow pace only geologists can detect. In satellite photographs of the Earth's surface, our continents and islands look like pieces of a giant jigsaw puzzle. These pieces could almost fit into one another.

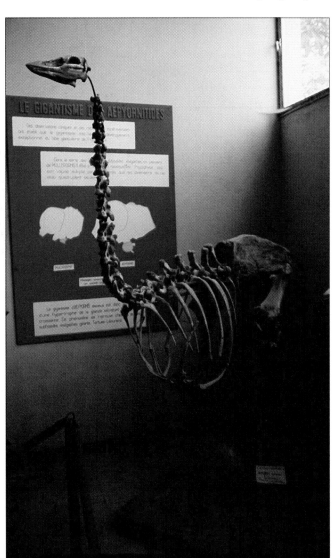

The skeleton of an *Aepyonis maximus,* an extinct bird of Madagascar, is displayed in a Malagasy museum.

During that ancient upheaval, a relatively small piece of land broke away from Gondwanaland. This narrow strip of land 976 miles (1,571 km) long drifted east into the Indian Ocean and is known today as the island of Madagascar.

As Madagascar moved slowly away from Gondwanaland, a shallow sea formed between the mainland and the island. At that time, about 165 to 180 million years ago, the waters were peaceful. Many mainland animals were able to cross the sea and find new habitats on the lush island.

Eventually, the island drifted farther away from the continent, and the sea between them became deeper and more difficult to cross. The creatures who had already reached Madagascar thus became isolated. With no new outside influences, they evolved in their own special ways. Likewise, some of the plant life that developed on the island resembles its cousins on the African continent, while other plants evolved into spectacular new forms. Today, approximately 75 percent of Madagascar's animal and plant species are unique to the island.

More than half of the world's 60 chameleon species live on Madagascar.

7

Some people believe the first settlers in Madagascar sailed over the Indian Ocean from Indonesia. They may have traveled in boats similar to the outrigger canoe in the picture.

Madagascar presently has a few inactive volcanoes. The only remnants of inner Earth activity are the hot springs and ash cones in the Itasy region of the highlands.

Like its amazing creatures and unusual landscape, Madagascar's people are also remarkably diverse. The population is made up of European settlers and an older community of Asian adventurers. The original settlers are divided into 18 ethnic groups. Each group has kept its unique identity, based on physical characteristics, oral history, and customs.

Even seen from space, the island is most unusual. In satellite photographs, Madagascar looks like a huge red strip in the Indian Ocean, almost as if the island were bleeding into the sea. Most of the island's soil is laterite—clay with a high iron content. Laterite quickly breaks down into loose red soil, which gave the island its nickname—the Big Red Island. Because of human carelessness, the rich red earth now washes into the surrounding waters.

As the morning sun rises above the trees at Berenty Reserve, the red soil of Madagascar becomes more apparent (right). In many areas, deforestation has caused the precious soil to be washed away into rivers and streams (inset).

Chapter Two

The Big Red Island

The footprint-shaped island of Madagascar is separated from the African continent by the Mozambique Channel. The Indian Ocean forms its eastern boundary. The island's southern tip is relatively round and wide, while its northern quarter gradually narrows to a point. This water-bound land boasts a variety of landscapes as great as most large continents. Madagascar has three major geographical regions: the high central plateau; the eastern coast; and the western coastal region and the southern desert areas. Landscapes range from high mountains to dry deciduous forests, savannas, rain forests, and finally to one of the most unique arid zones in the world.

The Highlands

The high central plateau, or highlands, rises from the broad lowlands on the west at an altitude of 2,500 feet (760 m) above sea level to an altitude of 6,500 feet (1,980 m) bordering the eastern coast. The highland plateau includes the three major mountain masses, called massifs. Formed from ancient volcanic activity, these mountains run from north to south in the center of the island and are rich in minerals and metal. Graphite, a mineral used for pencils, paints, and lubricants, is one of Madagascar's exports. Also found in the highlands are chromite, gold, mica, phosphates, and several types of semiprecious stones, such as agate.

The northern massif, called Tsaratanana, includes Maromokotro Peak, the highest point on the island. Maromokotro reaches a height of 9,436 feet (2,830 m).

Ankaratra Massif lies in the middle of the island. Its rugged cliffs and deep valleys offer spectacular scenery. Farther south is Andringitra Massif.

Madagascar's land regions and climates are full of contrasts. Mountains and abundant water (above) in one region become dry desert with strange looking plants in another (right).

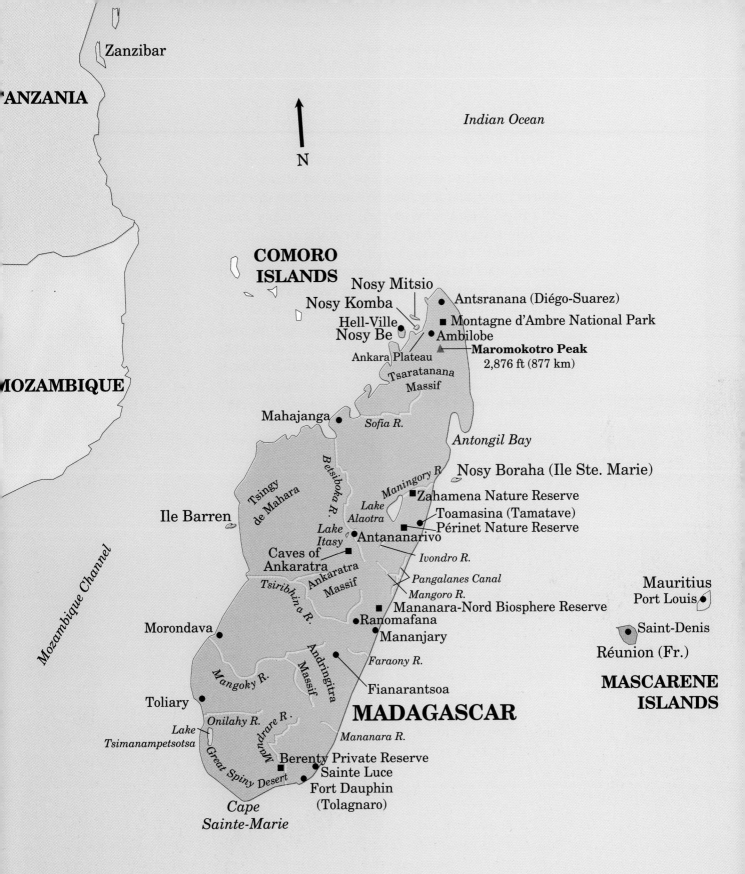

Zanzibar

TANZANIA

Indian Ocean

N

MOZAMBIQUE

**COMORO
ISLANDS**

Nosy Mitsio

Nosy Komba

Hell-Ville

Nosy Be

Antsranana (Diégo-Suarez)

Montagne d'Ambre National Park

Ambilobe

Maromokotro Peak
2,876 ft (877 km)

Ankara Plateau

Tsaratanana
Massif

Mahajanga

Sofia R.

Antongil Bay

Nosy Boraha (Ile Ste. Marie)

Maningory R.

Betsiboka R.

Tsingy
de Mahara

Ile Barren

Lake
Alaotra

Zahamena Nature Reserve

Toamasina (Tamatave)

Périnet Nature Reserve

Lake
Itasy

Antananarivo

Caves of
Ankaratra

Ankaratra
Massif

Ivondro R.

Pangalanes Canal

Mangoro R.

Tsiribihina R.

Mananara-Nord Biosphere Reserve

Ranomafana

Morondava

Mananjary

Andringitra
Massif

Faraony R.

Mangoky R.

Fianarantsoa

MADAGASCAR

Toliary

Onilahy R.

Mandrare R.

Mananara R.

Lake
Tsimanampetsotsa

Berenty Private Reserve

Great Spiny Desert

Sainte Luce

Fort Dauphin
(Tolagnaro)

Cape
Sainte-Marie

Mozambique Channel

Mauritius
Port Louis

Saint-Denis

Réunion (Fr.)

**MASCARENE
ISLANDS**

Indian Ocean

MADAGASCAR
▲ Mountain peak
■ Nature reserve or park
● City or town

The northern highlands also have unusual land forms known as *tsingy*. These eerie yet beautiful stone formations look much like moonscapes. The *tsingy* are rugged ranges that resemble steeples clustered together. They were carved out of limestone by the eroding action of wind and water. *Tsingy* means "to tiptoe" in Malagasy, which one must do on the steep slopes. These razor-sharp spires can reach a height of 656 feet (200 m). Like the high walls of medieval castles, they keep intruders out and shelter the inhabitants.

Within the deep gorges created by the stone cliffs lie secluded micro-ecosystems, visible only from afar. There are forests that no human has set foot in, caves that no one has entered or explored, and rivers with fish that have never known a hook or spear. This protected environment is one of the few places on Earth that has not been disturbed by humans. To this day, it has kept its original beauty and innocence.

Flatter lands lie at the base of the mountains. About 85 percent of Madagascar is covered with grassland called savanna, bamboo, and small trees like the traveler's palm. Much of the savanna lies

Limestone pinnacles known as *tsingy* can be 656 feet (200 m) tall in Tsingy de Maraha, a protected reserve in northern Madagascar.

The Malagasy use zebu cattle, a species familiar in Africa and Asia. The animal has a large hump on its back and a large piece of skin hanging from its neck.

in the central plateau. On these grassy plains, Malagasy herders raise zebu cattle.

Cattle herders periodically burn sections of the savanna in order to allow new grasses to take root. Rice farmers also clear hillsides and valleys in this manner. Burning enriches the soil and allows new seeds to take root. However, overuse of this technique can drain nutrients from the soil, making it less fertile. Soon, the soil is unable to support new growth. Without plant roots to hold it in place, the soil is vulnerable to erosion by wind or rain.

The central highlands are drier and cooler than the coasts. The weather is moderate with an annual rainfall of about 40 to 60 inches (101 to 152 cm). The hot, rainy season—from November to April—brings daily showers and frequent storms. Clouds accumulate in the valleys during the cool nights and dissipate over the mountains in the morning sun. The change in temperature creates updrafts and winds, but the days are usually pleasant and warm. Rain often falls in the late afternoon and evening. The air is humid, even during the dry season.

Rolling hills, grassy slopes, and numerous valleys can be found in the central highlands—one of the island's major farming regions. Major crops include cassava and rice, and coffee, cloves, and vanilla are raised for export. Malagasy farmers have not been able to produce enough food for the growing population, so Madagascar has been forced to import basic food products.

Unfortunately, many highland areas are no longer fertile due to misuse of the land by the ever-increasing human population. During the rainy months, the highlands may appear lush and green, but life seems to exist only along riverbanks during the dry season.

In the higher regions, swampy plains have formed in bowl-shaped alluvial depressions. The rugged landscape includes many lakes. Seven major rivers rise in the highlands and flow down to the east and west coasts.

Many varieties of rice are grown on Madagascar. It is the dominant crop.

The East Coast

The eastern coastal region of Madagascar—a strip of land about 30 miles (50 km) wide and 1,000 miles (1,609 km) long—is bordered by the Indian Ocean on the east and the craggy central highland cliffs to the west.

The east coast rivers, such as the Faraony, the Mananara, the Ivondro, and the Maningory, are short and difficult to navigate. They empty into coastal lagoons or tumble into the Indian Ocean over rapids and waterfalls. Madagascar's major port city, Toamasina (also called Tamatave), lies on the east coast at the mouth of the Ivondro River.

Eastern Madagascar is primarily a tropical rain forest. Summer temperatures average about 85°F (29°C). The rainfall is heavy due to monsoons and trade winds. This coastal strip receives from 80 to 116 inches (203 to 295 cm) of rain during the long rainy season. Even the cool and so-called dry season brings precipitation.

Coral reefs line the eastern coast, and strong winds make the ocean's waters dangerous. In the lagoons protected by the reefs, the French created sheltered harbor areas by building the Pangalanes Canal. Ships now have a continuous, safe passage along the coast.

Short rivers with rapids and waterfalls run toward the coast through the eastern region.

Rain forests cover the narrow strip of land along Madagascar's eastern coast.

14

The West Coast and the Southern Desert

Madagascar's west coast borders the Mozambique Channel. Although there are sand dunes and mangrove swamps, this region is basically a vast, open plain that was once covered by millions of trees. Except for a few stands, the trees are gone now, as land was cleared for farming. The sheltered basins and coves of the west coast, especially in the north, provide many ports for the island.

Small volcanic islands lie off the west coast of Madagascar. Nosy Komba (left) is one of the smaller islands that tourists can visit.

Small volcanic islands are located off the west coast. The largest are Nosy Be, Nosy Mitsio, and Ile Barren. The smaller islands are often used for scientific study and exploration. As on the east coast, coral reefs can be found offshore.

The western coastal region, extending up to 120 miles (190 km) inland, has sand dunes, mangrove swamps, and wide, open plains. The rivers of the west coast—including the Sofia, the Betsiboka, the Tsiribhina, the Mangoky, and the Onilahy—are longer and more navigable than those on the east coast. These rivers deposit huge loads of fertile sediment on the western plains. These vast plains, once covered by millions of deciduous trees, are now excellent farmland. The northwest section is especially fertile.

The west coast (leeward side) of the island is much drier than the east coast (windward side) or the highlands. The wind blows rain clouds across Madagascar from the east, dropping precipitation along the way and leaving the west coast much drier. Its rainy season is the shortest of the island's three regions.

As the land rises to the south, the climate becomes even drier. Just as the west coast receives

Very little rain falls in the Great Spiny Desert of southern Madagascar. Drought-resistant plants, such as leafless thorn trees, are unique to the island.

little moisture from the ocean winds, the southern tip of Madagascar remains relatively untouched by eastern storms. As a result, much of this area is desertlike. Only about 15 inches (38 cm) of rain fall annually, and most rainfall seeps quickly into the thirsty soil. Because the south has no mountains to trap moist air, what little water remains in the air evaporates quickly and is swept west by the winds.

Madagascar's varied landscapes have provided a sheltered environment for wondrous plants, strange animals, and diverse groups of people. But today's landscape is a pale shadow of what once existed in Madagascar. The future of the Big Red Island depends upon the ability of the Malagasy people to balance the demands of progress and preservation.

Chapter Three

The People Who Came to Paradise

Some historians disagree about the dates when African tribal groups first arrived in Madagascar. Others dispute the exact ocean route taken by the first Indonesian settlers. However, most experts agree that human beings first came to the shores of Madagascar between 1,500 and 2,000 years ago. Much like the animals that evolved into new and different species, these early settlers formed their own unique cultures.

According to a study published by American University in Washington, D.C., it is generally thought that Madagascar's first people were:

"...sailors whose route and motivation may never be known, although it is clear that a majority were not from neighboring Africa. Instead it is generally presumed that they were Indonesians who crossed the 6,000 miles of Indian Ocean, following the monsoon trade winds in outrigger canoes. These early sailors possibly crossed directly but more likely in stages, sailing first along well-established routes to India, thence to the Horn of Africa, and along the East African coast to Zanzibar, the Comoro Islands, and

Early settlers were carried by the trade winds across the Indian Ocean from Indonesia to the shores of Madagascar.

Madagascar. They may have included Africans or persons of mixed Indo-African descent who had been assimilated into their culture from earlier and as yet undiscovered settlements along the East African coast."

Original Inhabitants

Madagascar's original inhabitants were called "Tompontany," a Malagasy name meaning "Masters of the Soil." They may have been *lakato,* or "true outrigger people," from the Malay Archipelago in Indonesia. Some of these early people may also have come from Africa.

The original inhabitants of Madagascar probably used outrigger canoes, similar to those shown in the picture, for transporting people and goods.

One of the earliest of the Tompontany tribes were a people called the Vazimba. They were not African, but probably black pygmies. They are also called "Manimba," or "Those With Power to Feed." This name led anthropologists to believe that they were farmers. The Vazimba were noted for their fine pottery.

Madagascar's original settlers were probably farmers, such as these rice workers outside present day Antananarivo.

The Tompontany soon began trading with the peoples of Africa and the Comoro Islands—a group of four islands in the Indian Ocean between Mozambique and Madagascar. The profitable trade brought more settlers to Madagascar. Some of the Bantu peoples of southern and central Africa intermarried with the Malagasy and moved onto the island they called "Izao Ambany Lanitra," or "This Beneath the Sky."

MARCO POLO AND MADAGASCAR

The Western world first may have become aware of Madagascar in the 1200s through the writings of Marco Polo, an Italian trader. Marco Polo may have been the greatest traveler of the Middle Ages. He was best known for his writings about the 17 years he spent in China and other parts of Asia.

Although Marco Polo never visited Madagascar, he heard tales of the island from Arab traders. He wrote that the island, which he called "Mogadishu," was one of the largest and most fascinating islands in the world.

Portuguese explorer Diogo Dias called the island St. Lawrence Island, but that name did not last. The country's present name may be a form of Marco Polo's name for the island. It may also have been derived from the names of tribes that inhabited the island during these early European explorations. The picture to the right shows a bay near Antsranana (Diégo-Suarez) where Diogo Dias explored.

Arab Traders

During the 900s, Arab traders began making occasional visits to Madagascar, which they called "Isle of the Moon." According to ancient manuscripts, these Arabs, or African Muslims, traded with the Malagasy at various places on the eastern coast. They traded cloth for spices and slaves. Perhaps their most important contribution was the first written accounts of the islands.

Until that time, Malagasy history and culture had been passed down through the generations orally by elders and storytellers. Some historians say the Arabs were the first people to try to write down the spoken Malagasy language. Others say that Malagasy was first written by Welsh missionaries. Today, the Malagasy language is principally Indonesian, with a mix of Bantu, Sanskrit (a language from India), Arabic, English, and French vocabulary elements. Malagasy is written with a 21-character alphabet.

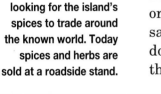

Early Arab traders were looking for the island's spices to trade around the known world. Today spices and herbs are sold at a roadside stand.

The Portuguese

In 1500, the first Europeans set foot on Madagascar. Captain Diogo Dias, a Portuguese explorer, was blown off course while sailing around the Cape of Good Hope. He was trying to discover a route to the Spice Islands.

Soon the Portuguese established a settlement on the southeastern coast and made several other colonizing attempts. Portugal's colonization efforts were abandoned because they could discover nothing of value for trade on the island, like gold, silver, or spices. However, the Portuguese did stay long enough to establish a slave trade.

Although many of Madagascar's people resemble Africans (such as the woman in the picture), they speak a language all their own. This confused the early explorers.

The French

After the Portuguese left, the French became interested in Madagascar. Joining in the race with other European nations to colonize new lands, France sent expeditions to the island to look for treasure. While the explorers found no treasure, they reported back to the French king about a strange island filled with unusual animals, strange monkeys, rivers running with blood, birds taller than men, and people who looked like Africans but spoke an unfamiliar language.

The word creole *was originally used in Latin America to describe the descendants of Spanish and French conquerors and native women. In Madagascar—a former French colony—creoles are a distinct group. Due to their mixed French and Malagasy ancestry, these people were often caught between two opposing sides of a political conflict. Most creoles were killed or driven out during a political uprising in 1947, which claimed more than 11,000 lives. However, some still live in areas of Madagascar like Nosy Be.*

Pirate Invasions to Colonization

In the waters just north of Madagascar, pirates and privateers ranged the Indian Ocean in the early 1800s. They used the nearby islands of the Republic of Seychelles as well as the harbors of Madagascar to hide from European ships. One of the most infamous privateers was William Kidd. Some people still believe that Kidd buried treasure on Madagascar, but no one has ever found it.

Dutch and French sailors came to Madagascar to trade arms for fresh water and food. The French, like the Portuguese, attempted to colonize the coasts. They established the settlement of Fort Dauphin (Tolagnaro) and Cape Sainte-Marie. But the Malagasy drove out the French.

At this time, the British became interested in the Big Red Island. During the 1700s and 1800s, Great Britain and France competed for trade and for converts to Christianity. The islanders grew accustomed

Hell-Ville market on the island of Nosy Be

THE DRONGO

The drongo, a bird endemic to Madagascar, developed into a unique sub-species. This bird has a forked tail and an unusual crest. It is most notable for its ability as a mimic.

Hundreds of years ago, the islands of the Indian Ocean were plagued by pirates. Madagascar was no exception. When pirates landed, the people normally gave a warning signal so that others could hide or move to a safer area.

During one of the pirates' attacks, a small group of women and children were separated from the main group and hid in a thicket of bushes. Just as the pirates were about to discover them, a baby's cry was heard nearby. The outlaws turned to follow the noise, but it moved farther away. Again and again the pirates followed the sound until it was finally heard coming from the treetops. The pirates looked up and saw a drongo. They had been fooled by a bird. Feeling silly, they left the jungle and went back to their boats.

The drongo had saved the lives of the women and children. Since that time, the drongo has been honored. It is *fady* (forbidden) to kill a drongo on Madagascar.

---

to the stopovers of European ships, and soon regular trading routes developed between Madagascar and Europe.

In the early 1800s, the European colonial powers came to an agreement that finally allowed the French to colonize Madagascar. After a period of resistance under Queen Ranavalona I, Malagasy society, religion, and government were gradually remade under strong European influence. A subsequent agreement allowed the French to declare Madagascar a protectorate in 1894 and then a colony in 1896. The French remained in control of the island until shortly after the end of World War II (1939–1945).

In 1958, after riots and demonstrations, the Malagasy formed their own government. In 1960, the island gained complete independence as the Malagasy Republic. In 1975, Madagascar took the first step toward a communist government. Didier Ratsiraka was approved as president under a new constitution that set up the Democratic Republic of Madagascar. After his victory, Ratsiraka solidified relations with other communist nations, as well as nationalizing banks, insurance companies, and natural resources.

After years of political unrest under Ratsiraka, a new coalition government was formed with Guy Razanamasy as prime minister and Albert Zafy as president in late 1991. The mission of the coalition was to smooth the transition between communism and a free market economy, and to draft a new constitution, which was finally written in 1993.

Daniel Defoe, an English writer best known for his novel Robinson Crusoe, *wrote a fictional account of a pirate republic on Madagascar called* Libertalia. *The novel probably was based on the life of John Plantain, a pirate who appointed himself king of Madagascar. No foreign government recognized the self-appointed king or his supposed queen, Eleanora Brown, as an official monarch.*

The Malagasy

While Europeans were trying to colonize the island, descendants of the first settlers were living out their own complex history. For the 18 ethnic groups on Madagascar, cultural identity today is based on the different kingdoms that flourished from the 1600s to the 1900s. It was not until the 1900s that all Malagasy groups came together as one people under French rule. Until that time, they were separated into smaller groups by variations in local dialect and geography. Today, they all share the same basic culture and speak the same language, but each ethnic group retains elements of its individual historical identity and dialect.

On Madagascar, rice is "the measure of all things." The Malagasy consume one pound (0.4 kg) of *vary*, or rice, per person per day, more than any other people except the Burmese. The traditional Malagasy people constructed their calendar accord-

The Malagasy do not usually question their Malayo-Polynesian origins. Although Madagascar is so close to Africa, Malagasy legends indicate that their ancestors came from Southeast Asia and Indonesia. The children in the picture reflect the mixture of ethnic groups.

A traditional trampling party is part of the ritual in preparing a rice field for planting.

ing to the distinct stages in cultivating rice, and the Malagasy vocabulary has many words relating to rice and its cultivation. Rice is also the basis for many conversations, stories, and sayings.

As melting snow represents time to the Inuit people of Alaska, the preparation of rice is a measure of time to traditional Malagasy. In his book, *A World Out of Time, Madagascar*, Frans Lanting wrote, "I once asked Rakotoarivo how far it was to a neighboring village. His answer was the number of pots of rice that could be cooked in the span it took to walk there."

Reverence for ancestors is also an important part of the Malagasy culture. In fact it is the primary focus of their spiritual beliefs. Andriamanitra ("The Perfumed Lord" or "The Creating King") or Zanahary ("The Creator") are two names for the one god. The Malagasy believe their ancestors, the *razana*, who live happily in "the beyond," have power over the daily lives of the living. The people believe that the *razana* will intercede with God for them, if they pray and give offerings of such things as meat, rum, or coins to the dead. In remote regions of the island, some Malagasy still sacrifice animals to the *razana*.

The Malagasy believe so strongly in the power

Rice seedlings are transported for planting in a dugout canoe.

23

of their ancestors that they never want to be far away from them. This explains why many tombs are half below and half above the ground, and why many people do not want to travel far from home. When a person dies, it is important to the Malagasy that the skull be buried beside the ancestor's tomb.

The people live close to the large stone tombs called "cold houses," because the ancestors are considered to be the originators and guardians of the traditional customs. Ritual funeral rites and highly decorated grave sites show reverence for the dead.

Famadihana is the practice of "turning over the dead." Traditionally, each winter (and now every four or five years because of the tremendous cost) the *mpanandro* (astrologer) declares that the time is right for a ritual in which the family tombs are opened and the bones removed.

The old *lambas* (cloths) are removed from the bones. The relatives then wash the bones and take them home, or tour the village with them, so their ancestors can see what has changed since they were last exhumed. The bones are then rewrapped in new silk cloth and placed in a setting of honor.

A huge festival completes *famadihana* as the people celebrate the reunion with the spirits of loved ones. There is a ritual slaughtering of zebu cattle, feasting, dancing, and speeches. The *valiha*, a stringed instrument, and lutes are played.

A typical Malagasy cemetery has many tombs aboveground.

Much of the island's history can be seen in the carvings on graves. These stone structures resemble totem poles that depict meaningful events from the lives of of the people buried beneath them. For example, above one chieftain's grave are figures showing the chieftain passing judgment on a villager. Below this another scene depicts his defense of a village family, and farther down a religious ceremony is portrayed.

Many Malagasy tombstones have elaborate stone carvings. Tombstones are more important and often more costly than Malagasy homes.

The Merina

The largest ethnic group on Madagascar is the Merina, or "People of the Highlands Where the View Is Wide." They live high on the island's central plateau. Hova, their language, is the most widely-spoken dialect on the island, although the official languages are Malagasy and French. Some people also speak a French dialect called Creole that began in the early days of slavery.

No one knows for certain where the Merina came from, but they probably arrived 700 or 800 years ago from Polynesia. The Merina became the dominant tribe on Madagascar in the late 1700s, eventually conquering the other tribes through war and intermarriage.

The Merina monarchy ruled Madagascar for 100 years until 1885, when they were defeated by the French. When the French abolished the island's monarchy, the last Merina monarch, Queen Ranavalona III, was exiled to Réunion, a French island 420 miles (680 km) east of Madagascar.

Today, the Merina form the largest segment of Madagascar's educated society. They are well represented in the middle class and intellectual elite as business people, professionals, technicians, and government officials.

These Merina men live in the central plateau region of Madagascar. They are hauling charcoal outside the capital city of Antananarivo in the central highland region.

RANAVALONA, QUEEN OF THE MERINA

Legend has it that when Queen Rana-valona, the widow of Merina king, Radama, came into power in 1828, she made it very clear that she was now in charge. Six days after her husband's death, while his body lay in state to dry out, she had all his other potential heirs put to death. The group included his designated heir, his other nephews, his half-brothers, his cousins, and even his mother. Ranavalona had them either strangled with silken cords or thrown in prison to starve to death. In this way she did not violate the rule that royal blood could not be shed.

The picture shows the queen's palace atop a hill above Lake Anosy in Antananarivo. This city is the Merina capital and also the capital of Madagascar.

The Betsimisaraka

During the late 1700s, the French established large plantations on several islands in the Indian Ocean, including the Comoros and Seychelles. Between 1769 and 1793, almost 40,000 Malagasy people were sent as slaves to work on these sugar plantations.

Port cities of Madagascar in this period thrived on the slave trade. As a major stop on the Indian Ocean sea-lane, the northeastern coast of the Big Red Island became known as "the old pirate coast." In addition to these easily accessible ports, trading communities had been established along the island's more hazardous lower east coast and in the small ports of the west. From the northeastern coast, European pirates plundered ships owned by the British East India Company and other shipping firms, particularly in the Mozambique Channel. The seafaring Betsimisaraka lived on the east coast of Madagascar and were easy prey for greedy slave traders.

During this time of European invasion, the Betsimisaraka—"The Many Inseparables" or "The Many Who Are United"—adopted their tribal name. Extremely good sailors, the Betsimisaraka united with the Merina in the late 1700s to fight the pirates and the French. They also became both sea raiders and slave traders. In particular, they stripped the

The people who live along the northeastern coast of Madagascar, the Betsimisaraka, are good sailors as their ancestors were.

nearby Comoro Islands of people and wealth until they themselves were defeated by the Portuguese in 1816.

Today, the Betsimisaraka are the second largest ethnic group on Madagascar. Of all the island's tribes, they are the most ethnically diverse. Their history is a result of two factors: their location in the coastal Toamasina area and their acceptance of immigrants from Indonesia, southern Asia, and the Arab states. Today, most of the Betsimisaraka are farmers on vanilla plantations and rice paddies.

The Betsileo

Sharing the highlands with the Merina, the Betsileo, or "Many Invincibles," make up the third largest ethnic group on the island. The highlands are good areas for raising cattle and cultivating rice. Numbering about one million, most of the Betsileo people live on the central plateau of Fianarantsoa, located between the capital city of Antananarivo and the southern provinces.

The Betsileo are expert farmers, cultivating the hilly terraces of the high plateau. These are similar to the rice terraces of Southeast Asian countries, their ancestral homeland. Quite often the soil is hard as cement. The people chase their zebu cattle in circles to break up the clods into soft and arable soil. This activity is fun for the Betsileo, but not so much fun for the cattle.

The Betsileo are believed to have come from Africa to Madagascar sometime during the 1400s. Like the Merina, they mixed with earlier residents, the Vazimba. The Betsileo also formed an alliance with the Bara, another of the major ethnic groups, through intermarriage. To this day, the Betsileo hold a favored position in Malagasy society. They are known as fine artisans, famous for their silk weaving and their wood carving.

The Betsileo use their zebu cattle to break up hard soil so it can be planted with rice and other crops.

The Tsimihety

The Tsimihety, or "The People Who Do Not Cut Their Hair," are descendants of several tribes—the Sakalava, Merina, Betsimisaraka, and Antakara. Like the Betsimisaraka, they may also be descendants of invading pirates, Arabs, and travelers from Zanzibar.

Their name is said to have come from a time when the Tsimihety honored a slain chieftain by refusing to cut their hair. In this way, the people showed that they would remain independent despite defeat by their enemies. Another explanation is less heroic. It suggests that Tsimihety men began to wear their hair long during the late 1800s so they would look more like women. The men would thus be in less danger of being killed by bandits.

The Tsimihety are the fourth largest ethnic group on the island. They have traditionally lived as seminomads in the north-central area of Madagascar. Unlike many other tribes, the egalitarian Tsimihety have always been a loose association of 40 kinship groups who believe that all people have equal political and social rights.

The Tsimihety are considered to be the most clannish, independent, and reserved of all the groups. They are also the most nomadic. They live in small, collectively working groups of farmers and cattle herders.

The Antandroy live in the dry regions of southern Madagascar.

The Antandroy

The Antandroy, or "The People of the Thorny Brambles," live a harsh, nomadic existence on the arid lands of Madagascar's southern tip. Of African origin, these tall, dark people tend the humpbacked zebu cattle that graze on the cactuslike plants of the desert. The zebu play an important cultural role in the lives of the Malagasy people.

The symbol of wealth and power, cattle are a

central part of the Antandroy culture. Until recently, stealing cattle was a rite of passage for young men. Even today a male must purchase his young bride with cattle.

Women have low status among the Antandroy and work very hard. In the early morning, they can be seen sponging dew off the succulent desert plants, in order to get enough water for their daily needs.

Several zebu cattle skulls adorn the gravestone of an Antandroy tomb.

Like all Malagasy, the dead have great significance in the daily lives of the living. The Antandroy believe in a spirit of influence called *Kokolampo*. Their tombs are rectangular and made of uncut stones that rise about 3 feet (1 m) above the ground. Zebu horns are used to decorate the graves.

Other Groups

A number of smaller ethnic groups make up the rest of Madagascar's population. The Antakarana on the northern tip of the island live by fishing and raising cattle. Because of the flooding waters, their houses are often on stilts. The Mahafaly in the desert of the southwest are artisans, farmers, and cattle-raisers. The Bara now live in the central south, raise cattle, and are noted for their dancing and wood carvings.

The Antaisaka, Antaimoro, Antanosy, Antaifasy, Antambahoaka, and Tanala peoples all live in the southeast. Two of these groups, the Antaimoro and the Antambahoaka, are of Arabian descent. Some still wear the traditional Arab robes and turbans, which are quite suitable for the island climate. The Tanala, or "People of the Forest," arrived on Madagascar only about 250 years ago. They live by fishing and, like many of the Malagasy, practice slash-and-burn farming methods. Unfortunately, large areas of their forested regions have recently been converted to large coffee plantations.

The Mahafaly live in the desert and raise cattle.

Chapter Four

Amazing Flora

From outer space, it may look like the world is on fire. Fire rages over the Earth's surface daily, destroying thousands of plant and animal species. An estimated 39 million acres (16 million ha) of tropical rain forests are consumed annually.

Madagascar is no exception. Fire destroys thousands of acres of the most unusual rain forest on Earth. Madagascar's rain forest has more endemic species than any other forest in the world. The island is like a special garden where people can observe the most beautiful and mysterious aspects of nature.

The diversity of life on Madagascar is nowhere more apparent than in the dwindling rain forests of the east coast. But the dry forests, savanna, and desert are equally important habitats.

Scientists estimate that 75 percent of Madagascar's plants and animals are endemic, or unique, to the island. These valuable plants and animals are now endangered by ax and fire. Yet, even as the forests are being destroyed, new species of plants and animals are being discovered. Perhaps one of these could be a plant that cures cancer or AIDS. Perhaps there is a species that could provide a high protein food for many of Earth's starving people.

This is not a pipe dream. It could happen, just as vaccines were discovered for smallpox and polio. Recently, several new varieties of palms were identified, and a mongoose that never had been classified before was found in Madagascar's southwest desert. Two new species of primates were found as recently as 1987. There are an estimated 100 million species on Earth, and scientists have only identified 1.4 million! Who knows how many of these species could be found on Madagascar.

The island's diverse ecosystems support a variety of plant and animal life. But all its natural environments have been drastically altered by people.

The flower of the ylang-ylang tree is used to make perfume.

"Ile Ste. Marie (Nosy Boraha) is botanically rewarding. Here you can see the spectacular comet orchid, Angraecum sesquipedale. The tubular nectary of this creamy-white flower is 38 centimeters (15 inches) long. When Charles Darwin was shown the orchid he predicted that a hawkmoth with a 38 centimeter (15 inch) tongue must exist in Madagascar to fertilise it. Sure enough; the moth is named praedicta, and the flower sometimes called Darwin's Orchid."
— Hilary Bradt in Guide to Madagascar, 1988

30

This banyan tree is in the dry rain forest of Madagascar. The branches of banyan trees send aerial roots to the ground below, growing new trees.

THE NATIONAL TREE

Madagascar's national tree is found throughout the land but especially in the Great Spiny Desert. A close relative of the banana tree, the traveler's palm (*Ravenala madagascariensis*) is a 30-foot (9-m) fan-shaped tree that looks like a palm. It got its name because a pocket at the leaf base holds a watery liquid. Travelers can get up to one pint (0.4 l) of this liquid by piercing the leaf stem. Then the pocket seals itself and refills.

Like many of Madagascar's trees, the traveler's palm is useful. Its tough leaves are 6 to 8 feet (1.8 to 2.4 m) long and are used for roof thatch. The leafstalks are used for house partitions. The seeds are a source of food, and the pulpy fiber around the seeds provides oil. The leaf also can be curled to make a spoon.

The traveler's palm appears on the official seal of Madagascar's. It is also depicted on the logo of the national airline, Air Madagascar.

The Special Nature of Trees

The trees of Madagascar have always held a strange fascination. In May 1990, Voahangy Rajaonah, a Malagasy geographer, wrote in the *Unesco Courier*, "The people of Madagascar believe that a place without trees is a place of infertility and death. A source of food and wealth, trees are also inhabited by invisible forces with which human beings must come to terms."

In spite of these beliefs, however, the islanders have decimated their forests and plains. They have cut down trees unmercifully and left a raw scarred land. And, in the process, they have brutally interfered with the habitats of Madagascar's extraordinary creatures.

At one time, Madagascar was almost all forest—broad-leafed evergreens in the rain forests, palms along the coasts, evergreens on the high plateaus, and strange and unusual trees in the dry south. Today, especially on the high plateaus, most of the trees are gone. They are the victims of too much slash-and-burn farming and the need for fuel and pastureland—the pressures of a rapidly growing human population. Up to 80 percent of the original forest cover on the island has been destroyed by human activity. American researchers have been using satellite images to document the destruction of Madagascar's rain forest. Clearly, the Malagasy have not yet found a balance between the need to preserve their natural environment for future generations and the desire to prosper today.

The three-cornered or triangular palm only grows in a 10-square-mile (27.2-sq-km) area of southern Madagascar.

The Great Spiny Desert

The southern portion of the island may have no rain for as long as nine months. In this cracked and parched land, strange deciduous trees—trees that lose their leaves—have developed. These trees have no leaves in the dry season, and their seedlings may grow only once in 5 years. This deciduous thicket is called the Great Spiny Desert, and 15 percent of the plants here are native to the island of Madagascar.

Tangled didierea form prickly sculptures as they twist and intertwine. And bottle trees stand as eerie sentinels in this strangely beautiful area.

Near the city of Toliary stands the fantsilotra, a tree with steellike spikes, 3 inches (7.6 cm) long, arranged in corkscrew patterns. A fall from this tree could mean certain death—not from the fall, but from the vicious spikes. The *Didierea trolli*, or "octopus tree," grows near the fantsilotra. This thorn tree, with branches that reach out like tentacles, secretes a sap that causes burns and even blindness. Looking somewhat like a tangled apple orchard, these trees form thorny thickets that few people dared enter until recently. Today, they are

The plants of the desert look very strange. The *Alluduaudia procera* is pictured at the far left. The inset shows the spines and leaves of the *Alluduaudia* plant. The *Euphorbia* tree is in the middle, and the *Didierea trolli* or octopus tree is on the far right.

The branches of the didiera or octopus tree look like tentacles with thorns.

Beautiful Grand Cascade Falls is located in the rain forest of Montagne d' Ambre National Park.

being cut down to provide wood for housing.

While the spiny desert is one of Madagascar's most unique landscapes, it is far from the only interesting area of vegetation. Madagascar's rain forest has a greater diversity of native species than any other rain forest on Earth.

The Rain Forest

The tropical rain forest is one of the most remarkable ecosystems on Earth. It not only provides its own humus and nutrient layer but also makes its own rain. All day long, thousands of gallons of water transpire, or escape into the air through the leaves, filling the atmosphere with moisture, and returning to Earth as rain. The trees in a tropical forest have a very shallow root system, due to the vast amount of moisture in the air.

Madagascar's evergreen forest is much more dense than other rain forests. It also has a lower canopy, with far fewer understory trees. And 80 percent of the plants in the Malagasy rain forest grow nowhere else in the world.

The Malagasy rain forest has a profusion of plant life. Broad-leafed evergreens and shrubs dominate. The epiphytes, or air plants that grow in the forest canopy, include ferns and 1,000 different varieties of orchids.

Many of the trees on the eastern slopes of the central plateau climb to over 100 feet (30 m). These trees, covered with vines and flowering plants, cling to the slopes and protect the forests below from erosion. The forest floor is carpeted with ferns, palms, and other protective ground cover.

Brilliant colors are everywhere. The vivid hues of orchids and other epiphytes wind along the treetops as their vines seek needed light.

Ninety percent of the eastern coast of Madagascar was once covered with rain forests. As the human population grew, it began to encroach on the forest. By the 1950s, the forest was about half of its original size. In 1985, well over two-thirds of the rain forest had been destroyed by human activities. Today, it is hoped that the Malagasy will preserve what remains of their ancient natural treasure through education and preservation.

The bird nest fern (top) and white orchids (bottom) are plants called epiphytes. They grow on other plants for support but do not feed off them.

The children of a small Malagasy village look as if they are being protected by the giant baobab tree behind them.

"Mother of the Forest"

To the southwest, near Morondava, stands a forest of water-gorged baobab trees, giants that can live for hundreds of years. The Sakalava people call the tallest of the baobabs *Reniala*, or "Mother of the Forest," because it rises above the other trees as if to protect and nourish them. Other Malagasy call it *Betroka*, or "The Big-bellied Mother of the Forest."

Baobab trees look strange because they appear to be growing upside down. The branches look like small wiry roots protruding at the top of the tree. The smooth gray trunk is large, thick, and bloated-looking. Some baobabs are 75 feet (23 m) in diameter and 60 feet (18 m) tall. Surprisingly, these giant trees have a very shallow root system.

According to legend, Zanahary, the Creator, was insulted by the baobab tree. So he punished it by turning it upside down, making the tree look foolish with its roots in the air.

Some Malagasy use baobab trees to bury their dead. Holes that develop in the trunks of older or dead trees are large enough to hold a body.

Apart from its reputation for harboring spirits, the baobab has many uses. Rope, paper, and cloth are made from the bark. The leaves provide seasonings and medicine. The pulp of its gourdlike fruit—sometimes called "monkey bread" or "sour gourd"—is edible and can also be made into an alcoholic drink.

Little has been done to protect the baobab. This forest, like the rain forest, is in danger of extinction. Most conservationists are predicting that all the forests in Madagascar could be destroyed within 35 years at the current rate of cutting. However, the government is now undertaking conservation and educational projects to preserve the forests. A massive reforestation effort is also underway.

The bark of the baobab can be made into rope, paper, and cloth.

Grasses of the Central Highlands

The hut of a slash-and-burn farmer in the Malagasy highlands

This region, with its mild tropical climate, once supported a mixed tropical forest filled with deciduous trees. Most of the ancient forests that covered the mountains, hills, and valleys have been cut down. Only remnants of this once magnificent ecosystem remain on the taller peaks and along some of the rivers.

Other large sections of the highlands were covered with succulent grasses that waved in the wind. They provided food for grazing animals, and their roots held the precious topsoil in place. In most areas today, these grasses have been destroyed by repeated burning.

Only isolated patches of the original grasses remain green and luxuriant, especially during the rainy season. These areas stand in stark contrast to the surrounding red and barren land where the soil is burned and overgrazed.

The Mangrove Swamps

Many rivers in the central highland flow west, emptying into the Mozambique Channel. Here in the tidal waters among the bays and channels, muddy lagoons, and river deltas, lie the mangrove swamps. The mangrove shrubs—small tropical evergreen trees—grow in dense thickets in the quiet saltwater lagoons. The mangroves are oddly beautiful. Their stiltlike roots plunge from their branches into the water, and their fruit hangs high above. The mangrove fruit is reddish-purple and tastes much like an orange.

There are three kinds of mangroves on Madagascar. All three reproduce by dropping their fruits into the water. The seeds often sprout while still attached to the tree. The heavy roots catch the dropping fruit and hold them upright in the muddy water until new plants are established.

Mangrove wood is hard and very dense. Consequently, it is not used for making furniture or for construction. But the trees are a good source of firewood. Their bark is often used in tanning leather and making dyes. Mangroves are also useful for fish farming, especially shellfish farming, because they provide natural shelters for breeding fish.

Safety in Numbers

No ecosystem can survive for long unless it meets certain ecological standards. For example, a

Clearing land by burning the vegetation is destroying the ecological balance on Madagascar. The picture below shows smoke rising from a fire set by farmers to clear land.

healthy community must be biologically diverse. Diversity in an ecosystem
helps prevent the spread of disease.
Sometimes bacteria, fungi, or insects
attack one specific species. But it is
much more difficult for a disease to
move from one specific species of
plants to another when these plants
are interspersed with hundreds of other
species. In this way, the more species there
are living together, the better their individual
chances of survival.

Genetic diversity is also important. Genetic dif-
ferences within a species strengthen the entire
species against disease, predation, and destruction
by other natural disasters. The weaker plants will
sicken and die when infected with a disease, while
those strong enough to survive will pass on their
defenses to the next generation. The survival of the
individual species within the larger community is
then ensured.

Maintaining Madagascar's diverse plant life is
not only important to humans but also to the
island's unique animal species. They cannot survive
without the special natural habitats the island
provides each species.

If the rain forests of
Madagascar are
destroyed, plants such
as the rosy periwinkle
may become extinct.
This plant is used to
make medicines to
treat certain kinds
of cancer.

Peasant farmers clear
land on the hills east
of the capital of
Antananarivo using
the slash-and-burn
method. Stopping this
kind of land practice
is important if
Madagascar is to main-
tain the biodiversity of
its plants and animals.

Chapter Five

From Tenrecs to Lemurs

The *Tenrec ecaudatus* found in southeastern Madagascar is the largest of the island's tenrecs.

Madagascar's isolation has produced a remarkable variety of peculiar creatures. Because of the island's remoteness, some of these strange animals have filled the niches occupied by other mammals on different continents. These adaptations are natural occurrences. When there is an empty space in nature, it begs to be filled—as it is on Madagascar.

The number of endemic species of wildlife on this island is unusually high. Almost all of its primates, 233 of its 250 reptiles, 131 of its 133 species of frogs, 8 of its 9 carnivores, and 29 of its 30 tenrecs are found only on Madagascar. Also, new species are discovered regularly.

Tenrecs

The primitive insect-eating, nocturnal tenrec, called *tandraka* by the Malagasy, is a hedgehoglike mammal with a long wet snout. Many tenrec species have quills and even look like miniature porcupines.

Scattered all over Madagascar, these small insectivores protect themselves with their bristles. Their quills are sharp and make a predator think twice before lunging. By moving their quills together, some tenrecs make an ultrasonic vibration that may be a means of communication.

The female tenrec holds the dubious distinction of having more nipples than any animal. She needs them, since she has litters of up to 30 babies.

Lemurs

Long ago lemurs lived on the African continent, evolving from the ancestors of primates about 58 million years ago. Scientists originally thought that when Madagascar broke away from the mainland, lemurs came, too. Isolated from the mainland and without natural predators, they didn't change and weren't replaced by other species.

This simple explanation has been discounted, however. Today scientists believe that the lemurs' early ancestors came from Africa as passengers on floating mats of vegetation. Even though the Mozambique Channel is wide, and crossing it would have been difficult, it is believed that there were probably two separate lemur crossings.

Lemurs are part of a very diverse mammal group called primates, belonging to the suborder *Strepsirhin*. (Humans, apes, and monkeys are also primates). There are 31 species and 50 different groups, or taxa, that share common characteristics. Before humans came to Madagascar, there were probably 15 more lemur species, now extinct

This mother and baby lemur (right) have pointed muzzles and large eyes, characteristics of all lemurs. They are generally gentle animals and friendly to humans (above).

because humans destroyed forest habitat.

These soft, furry creatures with long tails come in different sizes and colors. Some resemble monkeys; others look like raccoons, squirrels, or mice. They have monkeylike faces with long muzzles and a well-developed sense of smell. Lemurs usually live in trees and eat leaves, fruit, birds and bird eggs, and small animals. Some lemurs are active at night, sleeping during the heat of the day with their heads in their arms and tails curled around their necks. Others are active during the day.

The world's second smallest primate—the hairy-eared dwarf lemur—reaches 5.5 inches (14 cm) long and was believed to be extinct. It was rediscovered by the German primatologist Bernhard Meier in 1989. Meier and Patricia Wright, an anthropologist at Duke University's Primate Center, had discovered the golden-bamboo lemur in 1986. Like the endangered giant panda of China, the golden-bamboo lemur eats bamboo shoots. It is thought to be one of the most endangered of all primates—there are only about 25 in existence.

The tiny mouse lemur is probably the smallest primate on Earth.

Ranging in size from 4 to 6 inches (10 to 15 cm) and weighing between 1 and 3 ounces (28 and 85 g), the nocturnal miniature mouse lemur is considered the world's smallest primate. The mouse lemur can be found only on Madagascar. It haunts the eastern rain forests, feeding on insects, berries, and other fruits. This tiny lemur has a huge brain in comparison to its size and can live more than 15 years.

One of the primary reasons that mouse lemurs are considered so important today is that, in the last 30 to 50 million years, they have barely evolved. They are considered to be the nearest living example of the now-extinct, original primates and are commonly referred to as "living fossils."

The ring-tailed lemur (left) is characterized by its long, bushy tale. This species is one of the most abundant and "popular" lemur species on Madagascar.

Some lemurs on Madagascar hibernate. They sleep for seven months of the year—from April until October—when food is scarce. During that time, they live off their stored fat, just as bears do. They do not wake up again until the food supply is more abundant.

The golden-crowned sifaka, another endangered lemur, was discovered in 1974 by Dr. Ian Tattersall. Scientists at the Duke University Primate Center determined in 1986 that this lemur was a new and unique species. Much of the golden-crowned sifaka's habitat has been clear-cut for the raw materials to make charcoal. Only a small part of its forest environment remains. Luckily, a local *fady* forbids hunting this unusual lemur.

Lemur societies are female-dominated, a fact that intrigues many scientists. The females are the leaders and aggressors. They make the mating choices.

An interesting factor of lemur female dominance is the small difference in size between male and female lemurs. Perhaps this similarity in size means that the females must be more aggressive in order to feed and protect their young.

Female lemurs are dominant. These black female lemurs (right) are about the same size as the male, making it possible for them to compete quite easily for food. Although lemurs are usually not active during the day, this sifaka lemur (below) looks as if it is dancing in the sunlight.

Very few lemurs are diurnal, or active during the day. The diurnal species include ring-tailed lemurs, sifakas, or "Man-in-the-Trees," indris, and black lemurs. These animals are not as easy to see as one would imagine, because they are well camouflaged in their natural environment and very shy.

One of the strangest of all lemurs is the black-and-silver aye-aye, often regarded by the Malagasy as evil or a harbinger of death. The aye-aye is a weird combination of body parts that seem to belong to a wide variety of unrelated species.

With its wide yellow eyes heavily outlined in black, plumed black tail, and batlike ears, the elusive aye-aye peers from a tree as it munches on coconut meat. The aye-aye is an omnivore, eating both meat and plants. It uses its keen sense of hearing to listen for bugs and grubs beneath a tree's surface. Once it has pinpointed the food source, the aye-aye uses its front teeth to gnaw through the bark like a beaver. This hole is very small, so the lemur uses its long, crooked middle finger to reach in and scoop out the meal. In this way, the aye-aye fills the niche of the woodpecker on Madagascar.

Much undeserved evil has befallen the aye-aye because of its supernatural reputation. An aye-aye seen near a village must be killed, or it is believed that death will certainly come to the village.

Today, the aye-aye is protected on the UNESCO reserve of Mananara-Nord, located on the eastern coast of Madagascar. Once on the verge of extinction, this magnificent creature has made a comeback. Aye-ayes are more numerous and widespread than previously believed. The increase in aye-aye sightings is probably due to increased awareness of the small, nocturnal creatures.

Lemurs live all over Madagascar in a variety of environments. Biologists are fascinated by the way this relatively primitive creature has managed to adapt to so many different habitats and niches usually occupied by more advanced primates.

Verreaux's sifaka is one of the largest lemurs on the island. A terrific jumper, Verreaux's sifaka can cover over 24 feet (8 m) in one leap. This primate of the southern forest looks like a teddy bear and spends its time in the tamarind and baobab trees, where it eats, sleeps, and plays. The Malagasy believe sifakas are sun worshipers, because they turn their heads to the sun as it comes up. Sifakas are named for the sound they make when frightened— a hissing "sefaakh."

One of the best-known and most-loved lemurs is the ring-tailed lemur. It has a black nose in a white foxlike face, big eyes, a short

Blue Devil, named after Duke University's men's basketball team, was the first aye-aye born in captivity, on April 5, 1992. He weighed 5 ounces (142 g) at birth. Blue Devil's mother was brought to Duke as part of a captive-breeding program, designed to replenish the island's dwindling population of aye-ayes. None have been sent back yet since the population is not large enough.

The Verreaux's sifaka looks like a lovable teddy bear (above). The elusive aye-aye lemur (left) peers over a tree branch.

45

body, long legs, pointed ears, soft gray fur, and is 2.5 feet (74 cm) tall. The ring-tailed lemur is characterized by its raccoonlike tail, which is as long as its body with white and black rings.

The ring-tailed lemur is not afraid of humans. Unlike other lemur species, it spends the majority of the time on the ground.

The ring-tailed lemur is highly sociable, spends more time on the ground than most lemurs, and lives in troops of anywhere from 5 to 35 members. An herbivore, the ring-tailed lemur subsists on the lush vegetation of the island's forests.

The largest type of lemur living today—the indri—is the size of a large raccoon, about 45 pounds (20 kg), and the only lemur that has no tail. The black-and-white, leaf-eating indri can be seen in the Périnet Nature Reserve. The indri is noted for its sad, haunting howls, which can go on for hours. At other times it makes an unbelievable noise, something like a crying child but much louder. This singing herbivore eats over 50 different kinds of vegetation, a major reason why no indri has survived in captivity.

The indri is the only lemur without a tail. The Malagasy believe this lemur's body resembles the human body.

The indri, like the aye-aye, is regarded by the Malagasy with superstitious reverence. The Betsimisaraka refer to the indri as *babakoto*, or "cousin to man," since their bodies look almost human. Some Malagasy believe that the souls of the dead must enter and pass through an indri before the soul can rest. One legend tells of a time when bandits approached a village, and the indris howled a warning. The bandits fled.

Traditionally, the people of Madagascar have believed that their fate was linked to that of the natural environment. An old fable says that once upon a time, an animal called the *babakoto* lived and prospered in

Malagasy mammals on the Endangered and Threatened Wildlife and Plants list include avahi, aye-aye, indri, and sifaka lemurs. Endangered reptiles include angulated tortoises and radiated tortoises.

the eastern rain forest. It lived on leaves and fruits and led a relatively easy life. This *babakoto* had four children. Two of the children remained in the forest and lived like their parents. The other two children left the forest and went to work as farmers on the land. These two children became the first ancestors of the Malagasy people. This is why it is *fady*, or forbidden, to hunt the *babakoto*, or indri. This tale, and many like it, are common in Madagascar's folklore and show the people's traditional close ties to the land. But somewhere along the way this feeling of closeness has been lost.

Other Mammals

Five orders of land mammals live on Madagascar—lemurs, bats, tenrecs and shrews, carnivores, and rodents. Like many of the lemurs, these mammals are very uncommon creatures.

Thirteen of Madagascar's 26 bat species are endemic. The rest probably fly back and forth to Africa across the Mozambique Channel. Like other mammals, bats have a variety of diets. Some are insect-eaters, and others, like the flying fox, or fruit

Flying foxes have facial features that resemble those of foxes.

bat, the most familiar species, are fruit-eaters. The flying fox has see-through wings, thick reddish-brown fur, large black eyes, a foxlike snout, and an amazing wingspan of 4 to 5 feet (1.2 to 1.5 m). The Malagasy say flying fox bats are delicious to eat because their diet consists of ripe fruit.

It is hard to imagine a bat more unusual than the sucker-footed bat. Like the aye-aye, it is the only species in its genus and the only genus in its family. The sucker-footed bat lives in the traveler's palm, near Ranomafana. It measures about 6 inches

(15 cm) from head to tail. Both the tail and the fore-arms are about 5 inches (13 cm) long. It has suction discs on its wrists and ankles which help it to grip surfaces. Little is known about the sucker-footed bat. Scientists can only assume it eats insects, but no one knows for sure.

Madagascar is home to carnivores (meat-eaters) as well. The mongoose, for example, is a reddish, minklike animal with a long ringed tail. It prowls the trees and ground for insects, worms, eggs, snails, chameleons, and small lemurs.

The largest of the carnivores is the fossa, the only creature on the island that hunts the larger lemurs. These expert tree climbers are the size of a large dog—about 70 to 80 pounds (32 to 36 kg). They have retractable claws, strong jaws, and a long tail that helps them balance in the trees.

The fossa also hunts the giant jumping rat, an animal that fills the niche of a rabbit on Madagascar. This 12-inch (30-cm) brown rodent has large rabbitlike ears. It hibernates in winter and hops like a kangaroo. The giant jumping rat was endangered to the point of extinction, but today a special reserve for these animals is located in the baobab forest near Morondava.

The ocean has many interesting mammals, including some of the largest ones on Earth. Whales, such as the blue whale, humpback whale, sperm whale, shortfin pilot whale, and the bottlenose dolphin, who are members of the whale or cetacean family, inhabit the waters of the Indian Ocean, particularly around Antongil Bay. The same area is home to the huge vegetarian dugong or sea cow. This great creature is almost extinct. The dugong is bluish-gray and has a deeply-notched tail. The dugong's body can grow to about 14 feet (4 m). Like the dolphin, dugongs are very gentle animals. When dugongs were plentiful, the Malagasy hunted them as a great delicacy.

In an effort to save large, warm-blooded aquatic mammals, the International Whaling Commission created the Indian Ocean Whale Sanctuary in 1979. This sanctuary protects aquatic mammals throughout the Indian Ocean. Today, 43 species of dolphins and whales live in Madagascar's protected ocean waters.

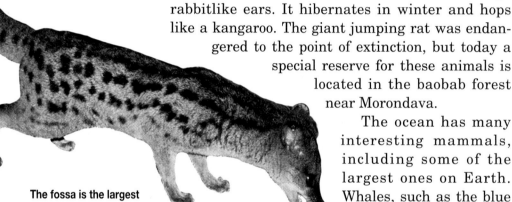

The fossa is the largest meat-eating mammal on Madagascar.

LEGEND OF THE CROCODILE

The crocodile is the fiercest carnivore on Madagascar. It has long played an important role in Malagasy tradition and legend.

"...the Zafandravoay ("sons of the crocodile") clan of the Antandroy people claim to be descended from the two sons of a woman who had married a crocodile. The Zafandravoay regard themselves as immune from attack by one of these reptiles, which they are at pains never to harm; their tribal dead are believed to turn into crocodiles after entombment and to go off to join their ancestors in the river. Other Madagascan tribes (the Antakara, the Sakalava, and the northern Betsimisaraka) all thought that the souls of their dead chiefs passed into the body of crocodiles, and in some places there was a tradition of human sacrifice . . . ."

— Rodney Steel in *Crocodiles,* 1989

Amphibians and Reptiles

One significant feature distinguished the first mammals from the reptiles who roamed Earth. Through a chemical reaction called endothermy, the mammals' bodies were able to absorb heat and raise their body temperatures. This allowed them to sleep during the day and hunt for insects and other prey at night.

Madagascar was once home to the giant crocodile, a beast that could swallow a person in the blink of an eye. Like the elephant bird, however, giant crocodiles are now gone forever. Today, Nile crocodiles exist in remote rivers and swamps, as well as underground. The subterranean crocodiles live in the caves of Ankarana, which has over 60 miles (96 km) of caves and a wide underground river. In this river, crocodiles over 13 feet (3.9 m) long spend the dry season.

Although the crocodile is the most fierce meat-eater on Madagascar today, other reptiles are also carnivores. For example, snakes are common on the island. One species, the do, or boa constrictor, reaches 10 to 15 feet (33 to 49 m) in length. A good climber, the boa constrictor eats small birds and mammals. Before swallowing them, it crushes the creatures in its mighty coils. The Betsileo believe that boa constrictors are their ancestors and treat them with great reverence.

Madagascar's most prolific reptile by far is the chameleon, a type of lizard that originated in Madagascar and eventually spread throughout the world. Chameleons are harmless to humans but not to insects, their primary source of food. Madagascar is home to 59 species,

The boa constrictor, or do, is powerful and crushes its victims before eating them.

representing two-thirds of the world's chameleons, including the largest and smallest varieties. The Malagasy believe that bad luck will follow a person who injures any chameleon, especially the world's smallest reptile, *Brookesia peyrierasi*, named after Malagasy naturalist Andre Peyrieras.

Chameleons are found primarily in Africa and Madagascar, but some live in the Middle East and Mediterranean islands. They have been around for millions of years. Most chameleons are arboreal—they live in trees and only come down to ground level to lay eggs or perform their courtship ritual.

The eyes of chameleons move independently of each other. They can look straight ahead and backwards at the same time. They not only see where they are going but also where they have been. Chameleons spend most of the day motionless. Sometimes they rock back and forth on a branch to look more like a leaf. The chameleon's prehensile tail is used for gripping branches. Its sticky abrasive tongue, used to catch a quick insect snack, is often longer than its body.

Many people think chameleons change color to suit their environment. But actually, chameleons change their color and pattern to suit their mood. The adaptation is due to a combination of light, temperature, and nervous stimulation.

Chameleons can change color. This is determined by temperature, light, and emotional factors, such as fright or victory in battle.

Although chameleons usually don't move much during daylight hours, they can travel very quickly when necessary.

While chameleons are talented camouflage artists, another lizard species—the leaf-tailed lizard or fringed gecko—found on Madagascar is the true master of deception. The fringed gecko (*Taha fisaka*) blends in so well with the trees that, even when it moves, it is almost impossible to see. The frilled gecko (*Uroplatus henkeli*) has an eye that looks like a peach stone. Legend says that contact with a gecko is fatal. It is said to pounce onto a person's body, particularly the chest area, where it sticks like glue. Once attached, these lizards can be removed only by cutting them off, causing a loss of skin and scarring. Some people believe that the only way to counteract the danger is to pierce the contaminated area and let the blood act as a purifier.

The gecko is camouflaged so well that it is difficult to tell where it ends and the tree starts.

The island is also home to five species of land tortoises. The geometrically designed radiated tortoise (*Testudo radiata*) waddles slowly across the parched landscape. Some Malagasy believe the tortoise brings good luck and attempt to protect it.

The largest tortoise, weighing up to 60 pounds (25 kg), is the ploughshare (Angonoka), which is also one of the rarest tortoises in the world. Only 200 to 400 ploughshares are thought to exist. Many tribes believe that a chance encounter with a ploughshare brings good fortune.

The spider tortoise is also endangered on Madagascar.

The ploughshare gets its name from the way the shell protrudes under the tortoise's head. During mating season, the male ploughshare uses this protuberance, called a gular projection, or an *ampondo*, by sliding it under the shell of his challenger and flipping him over onto his back. The victor gets the female.

Butterflies and Moths

Approximately 300 species of butterflies and moths live on the island. Of these, 233 species are endemic. Among the various species is a swallowtail, with relatives in India; the uranid moth; and the graceful comet (*Argema mittrei*)—one of the largest moths in the world, with a wingspan of about 8 inches (20 cm). Its larvae develop in a spectacular silver cocoon.

Unlike their relatives in the United States, Madagascar's moths are more brilliantly colored than its butterflies. Butterflies can be distinguished from moths by the clubbed tips of their antennae. Most types of moths also have an extra pair of eyes called ocelli. The reddish-gold, green, and black day-flying moth (*Chysidia madagascariensis*) is considered to be the most dramatic of all the world's moths and butterflies.

The pitcher plant is carnivorous, preying on Madagascar's insects.

Other Insects

Spiders, dragonflies, and wasps, like insects everywhere, are plentiful in Madagascar. The numerous termites build large nests, and millipedes scurry along on their multitudinous legs. Some types of mosquitoes—there are 20 different species on Madagascar—are so ferocious that insect spray doesn't keep them from biting, and netting doesn't stop them from drawing blood.

Millipedes are found worldwide, but they are quite large in Madagascar.

Swarms of horseflies, grasshoppers, and cicadas add to the endless whirring, chirping, buzzing, and humming.

The ant lion is a rather ugly little insect with large antennae. The larvae, called doodlebugs, live in conelike holes that they dig with their long, sicklelike jaws. The larvae trap and eat ants and other insects.

Birds

Aepyornis maximus, or *vorombe,* which means "big bird," was Madagascar's most fascinating bird. Also known as the elephant bird because of its elephantine legs, this land-dwelling creature was once the world's largest bird. It stood between 9 and 10 feet (2.5 and 3 m) tall and weighed more than 1,000 pounds (450 kg). Unfortunately, all that remains of this giant creature are millions of broken egg shells and, once in a while, a whole egg, weighing up to 20 pounds (9 kg) and containing a preserved embryo.

The elephant bird has been gone for several hundred years, but Madagascar is still home to some marvelous bird life. There are approximately

There are 1,200 different species of cockroaches on the island, mostly tropical. In 1989, the hissing cockroach of Madagascar became a pet fad started by an exotic pet store in Tampa, Florida. It sold for $6. When four were set free, people worried that they would rapidly multiply—so far there is no evidence that they have. Hissing cockroaches can live as long as 5 years.

The *Aepyornis maximus* was a large flightless bird. Its football-sized eggs can still be found in Madagascar, although the bird has been extinct for several hundred years.

250 species of birds, of which 125 are endemic. The songs, screeches, and trills of these birds fill the air. Each species has its distinctive feathers, coloring, and melody.

A cuckoo living in the Great Spiny Desert serenades the barren landscape. Believing the cuckoo has magical powers, some people use the bird's eyes and wing feathers to make a love potion.

Many other kinds of birds are found on the island, including the noisy ugza black parrot, white-eyed and yellow-headed weavers, warblers, Asian and magpie robins, and partridges. There are also egrets, pigeons, button quail, coucals chirping "cou-cou-cou," helmet birds, the mimicking drongos, herons, doves, hawks, and many others.

Not all birds on Madagascar live there year-round. Across the Red Sea and Horn of Africa, Eleanora's falcon leaves its summer home on the cliff tops of the Mediterranean to winter in Madagascar. Near the waters of Lake Tsimanampetsotsa, thousands of migratory white and pink flamingos nest and breed.

The crested coua is found only in Madagascar.

Fish

The ocean waters of Madagascar also hold links to times gone by. The coelacanth, sometimes referred to as a "living fossil," is a primitive fish. Until 1938, when one was caught by some South African fishermen, scientists thought it had been extinct for about 50 million years. Paleontologists believe the coelacanth might be an ancestor to some land animals.

The coelacanth lives in the depths of the ocean. It is 6 feet (1.8 m) long and weighs approximately 150 pounds (68 kg). Its scales are bluish-gray, and

its spines are hollow. The coelacanth has flourished in the Earth's waters for 75 million to 300 million years. Today, this ancient fish can be found only in the waters off the island's west coast.

In the Ankara plateau, close to Ambilobe in the north, blind white cave fish live in the huge underground cave system. Vision and color are useless in the lightless environment of the deep caves, so the animals who live there lose the ability to see and are either colorless or transparent.

However, all these fascinating creatures pale in comparison to the tremendous variety of fish and animals in the coral reefs off the coast of Madagascar. The reefs in the Indian Ocean are said to surpass even the Great Barrier Reef off the coast of Australia in population density.

Madagascar's wildlife faces tremendous odds against survival. Because the human population is growing so quickly, much of the land has already been stripped of vegetation and no longer provides enough food and protection for the native animals. How can the land regain its ability to support all of its inhabitants?

The coelacanth first appeared over 350 million years ago. This "living fossil" was thought to be extinct until one was caught in 1938.

This large sisal plantation in south Madagascar is located on land that was cleared of its natural vegetation. As more and more land is cleared, the island's animals are losing critical habitat.

54

Chapter Six

The Future

Can people learn to better understand and care for the wonders of the natural world? The government of Madagascar is attempting to answer that question.

Madagascar has joined in the worldwide struggle to protect the environment. Its people are spearheading the search for a workable policy to save some of the planet's dwindling natural resources.

Madagascar was one of the last large landmasses colonized by humans. The early settlers brought the ways of their original cultures. Some of these practices proved devastating to the Big Red Island.

From Asia, people brought farming techniques and agricultural practices that worked well on larger landmasses but turned out to be unsuitable for an island with limited space. The terraced fields and rice paddies, as well as the vast pastures needed for grazing cattle, soon took over the land required to support the island's original plant and animal life.

While Madagascar may still be one of the most biologically rich areas on Earth, its plants and animals may also be the most endangered in the world. Future generations may have to go to zoos to see these unique animals.

Up in Flames

According to Malagasy legend, a fire once raged in the center of the island and burned without end. The flames ate away at the surface until only the bare skeleton of the land remained.

Madagascar's central plateau has been stripped bare of vegetation.

While this story is merely a simple legend, it comes uncomfortably close to the reality faced by the 13 million residents of Madagascar today. The world's environmentalists are working with the government of Madagascar to preserve what remains of the forests on the island.

The Malagasy farmer and herder each need good fertile land if they and their families are to survive. Taking a risk on a new farming technique also means risking the lives of their families. Few are willing to break with the traditions of centuries.

The use of traditional agricultural techniques has dramatically altered the face of the country. At one time, forests covered most of the island. Now less than 25 percent of Madagascar is forested. Fires meant to renew the savanna now rage out of control, destroying valuable forestland. Over the past 40 years, deforestation has resulted in the loss of 272,000 acres (110,000 ha) per year. Stripped of its protective vegetation, the land is riddled with gullies and red with erosion.

Slash-and-burn farming techniques are sustainable only when practiced by small numbers of people with a large forest area available to them. These same techniques become harmful when the population grows. Overused, the soil becomes less fertile and unable to support much plant life.

Cattle herders may burn a section of savanna in order to renew it. Without the tall, dry grasses blocking the sunlight, new seedlings can take advantage of the nutrients in the ash and will grow quickly. Cattle prefer the tender green shoots to the mature, dry grasses. However, this renewal process, like slash-and-burn farming, can be overused. Prairie fires are extremely difficult to control, often damaging forestland, as well as savanna.

Without the root systems of trees and grasses to hold the soil in place, the island's fierce rainstorms, violent cyclones, and strong winds result in rapid erosion. As the soil washes away, the land looks more like a desert than a paradise. The giant red ring in the ocean surrounding the island, as seen from space, is made up of valuable soil.

Severe erosion near Antsranana (Diégo-Suarez) is washing away precious topsoil.

The forest has been cut down right up to the end of Montagne d'Ambre National Park.

Finding the Balance

Nowhere on Earth is the struggle of people with their environment more apparent. It is estimated that as much as 80 percent of the country's original forest cover has been destroyed or converted by people. Madagascar's population is one of the fastest-growing in the world and is expected to double by the year 2015. As the demands of human life increase, the available land decreases.

The only true wilderness left lies on the perimeter of the island. Described by Alison Jolly as a "string of pearls" in her book, *World Like Our Own*, this untouched region is the last area of its kind on Madagascar.

Because of its rugged nature, much of this land is unsuitable for agriculture or grazing and practically inaccessible for research and exploration. Two of these areas are *tsingy*, huge jagged limestone massifs in the northern and western areas. Beneath the sharp pinnacles of this untouched land lies a maze of unexplored caves and passages. However, the continued existence of these areas does not change the situation as a whole.

"Conservation for Development"

What can be done to preserve the remaining flora and fauna? Without their special habitats, they will soon disappear. Any ecological solution depends in part on the government.

With an ever-growing population, the citizens of Madagascar are struggling to meet their daily needs. The picture shows market day in a small village in Madagascar's central plateau.

Morning light shines on the Mandrare River in the Berenty Reserve in southern Madagascar. This reserve is the one most often visited by tourists and Malagasy. It is owned by the de Heaulme family.

Some reserves and parks have already been set up to preserve and protect the natural environment. By 1934, eleven natural reserves were established. By law, the plants and animals in the reserves are completely protected. They represent a cross section of the island's unique wildlife. The problem with the reserve system lies in enforcing its protective status. The government lacks the funding and resources to adequately patrol the areas and to enforce compliance with the laws.

The solution also depends in part on the people of Madagascar. They must be willing to learn about conservation and preservation. And they must find less destructive methods of farming, fuel use, and grazing.

Luckily, the rest of the world is willing to help preserve the Big Red Island. Madagascar has already benefited from creative techniques like the debt-for-nature swap pioneered by Conservation International in Bolivia in 1987. Under these plans, conservation groups buy part of a country's debt and swap it for environmental projects.

The Zahamena Nature Reserve is located in east Madagascar. Comprised of lowland tropical forest, it is home to 11 lemur species.

In 1985, Madagascar was host to an international conference to discuss conservation for development. The major purposes of the conference were to develop methods for managing the island's natural resources and to help Madagascar become self-sufficient in terms of food and fuel production. These goals require there must be a cooperative effort between the island's systems and the world community. A combined effort by international conservation, development, and assistance organizations has begun that will lead the way toward saving the environment of Madagascar and stabilizing its economy.

In 1989, the Mananara-Nord Biosphere Reserve was created as a part of the UNESCO Man and the Biosphere Program. This 54,050-acre (140,000-ha) reserve includes two national parks, a marine park, and a multiple-use area. The largest threats facing this reserve are continued use of slash-and-burn agricultural techniques, overuse of timber for construction, and hunting of endangered species for food. Since the project began, UNESCO reports a decrease in the destruction of the forest. They accomplished this goal by trading education and aid for the promise of preservation.

More recently, Madagascar worked with the United Nations Development Program (UNDP), the World Bank, and the governments of the United States, Switzerland, Germany, and Norway, to create Environment Program 1 (EP1). EP1 is an attempt to develop international cooperation and support for the first stage of a 15 to 20 year program called the National Environmental Action Plan (NEAP). This plan has seven main components, one of which is biodiversity conservation. Under this particular component, laws protecting many of the island's existing parks and reserves will be strengthened, and some new reserves will be created.

The key to protecting Madagascar's unique environment is educating people. Ecotourists (below) come to Madagascar to learn more about its unique environment. Many environmental organizations sponsor such trips.

The government of Madagascar has finally realized that much of the island's future lies in immediate improvement of its environmental systems. The government now realizes that natural habitats must be strictly preserved to protect the rare creatures that make their land so special.

Madagascar has enough fertile earth and resources to feed its people if the people begin to reduce the rate of population growth. Family planning needs to be a part of the overall conservation effort.

With the population in check, the islanders could easily feed themselves by using agricultural techniques that are ecologically sound. With proper management, the forests still standing could support wildlife and also supply fuel.

The unique flora and fauna of Madagascar can still be saved, but time is running out. The Malagasy people must learn from the past in order to create a vision for the future. Perhaps the new emphasis on conservation and preservation will bring a renewed respect for nature. Only a firm commitment to its natural wonders can stop the Big Red Island from bleeding its life into the Indian Ocean.

Two of Madagascar's unique plant species, the baobab and didierea, are silhouetted at sunset.

GLOSSARY

biological diversity – a variety of species living within the same ecosystem.

clear-cut – stripped bare of all trees, bushes, and other growth. Clear-cut land is usually burned after it is cut.

Cretaceous period – the last geologic period of the Mesozoic era, during which dinosaurs disappeared, and flowering plants developed.

ecosystem – a specialized part of the biosphere. It supports plant and animal life in an interdependent balance with nonliving aspects of the environment.

endemic – belonging to a particular location.

endothermy – a chemical reaction that causes mammals' bodies to absorb heat, enabling them to raise their body temperature so that they can sleep during the day yet maintain a high body temperature at night.

evolution – in biology, the development of a species, organism, or organ from its original or simple state into its present or complex state.

extinct – when there are no longer any living members of a given species.

fady – forbidden, in Malagasy.

fertile – able to support life.

genetic diversity – the existence of a variety of different genes within a species.

geologist – a person who studies the history of the Earth, especially as recorded in fossils and rock formations.

habitat – the specific environment of a plant or animal, including soil, weather, landforms, and other living things.

Jurassic period – the second period of the Mesozoic era, during which dinosaurs flourished, and primitive mammals and birds first appeared.

larva – the newly hatched form of an insect before metamorphosis when the insect has no wings. plural: larvae

Malagasy – of or belonging to Madagascar. For example, "the Malagasy people."

mammal – any group of animals that have a backbone and feed their young with mother's milk.

mantle – the layer of molten (liquid) rock that lies just below the Earth's surface.

privateer – a ship and crew that are licensed by a government to plunder enemy ships.

reptiles – any of the class of air-breathing, scaly vertebrates (animals having backbones or spinal columns).

zebu – a cowlike animal with a large hump over the shoulders, short curving horns, and a large loose fold of skin hanging from the throat. The zebu subsists by grazing.

FOR MORE INFORMATION

Books

Attenborough, David. *Bridge to the Past, Animals and People of Madagascar*. New York: Harper Brothers, 1961.

Bradt, Hilary. *Guide to Madagascar*. Bucks, England: Bradt Publications, 1988.

Durrell, Gerald. *The Aye-Aye and I, A Rescue Mission in Madagascar*. New York: Arcade, 1993.

Hargreaves, Dorothy and Bob. *African Trees*. Kailua, Hawaii: Hargreaves, 1972.

Kent, Raymond K. *Early Kingdoms in Madagascar, 1500-1700*. N.p.: Holt, Rinehart, and Winston, 1970.

Lanting, Frans. *Madagascar, A World Out of Time*. New York: Aperture, 1990.

Madagascar...in Pictures. Visual Geography Series. Minneapolis, Minn.: Lerner, 1988.

Murphy, Dervia. *Muddling Through in Madagascar*. Woodstock, N.Y.: Overlook Press, 1985.

Nelson, Harold D., Margarita Dobert, Gordon C. McDonald, James McLaughlin, Barbara Marvin, and Philip W. Moeller. *Area Handbook for the Malagasy Republic*. Foreign Area Studies. Washington, D.C.: American University, 1973.

Newitt, Malyn. *The Comoro Islands, Struggle Against Dependency in the Indian Ocean*. Boulder, Co.: Westview Press, 1984.

Steel, Rodney. *Crocodiles*. Bromley, England: Christopher Helm Publishers, 1969.

Stevens, Rita. *Madagascar, Places and Peoples of the World*. New York: Chelsea House, 1988.

Veevers-Carter, Wendy Day. *Island Home*. New York: Random House, 1970.

Wilcox, Robert. *Madagascar & Comoros, A Travel Survival Kit*. Victoria, Australia: Lonely Planet Publications, November 1989.

Wilson, Peter J. *Freedom by a Hair's Breadth, Tsimihety in Madagascar*. Ann Arbor: University of Michigan, 1992.

Periodicals

Endangered and Threatened Wildlife and Plants, 50 CFR 17.11 & 17.12. Washington, D.C.: U.S. Department of the Interior, U.S. Fish and Wildlife Service, Division of Endangered Species, August 29, 1992.

Jolly, Alison. "Madagascar: A World Apart." Washington, D.C.: *National Geographic*, vol. 171, no. 2, pp. 148-183, February 1987.

Marden, Luis. "Madagascar, Island at the End of the Earth." Washington, D.C.: *National Geographic*, vol. 132, no. 4, pp. 443-487, October 1967.

Rajaonah, Voahangy. "The Sacred Trees of Madagascar." *UNESCO Courier*, May 1990.

Wetmore, Alexander. "Recreating Madagascar's Giant Extinct Bird." Washington, D.C.: *National Geographic*, vol. 132, no. 4, pp. 488-493, October 1967.

Videos

Living Planet. S.C. Johnson, 1979.

INDEX